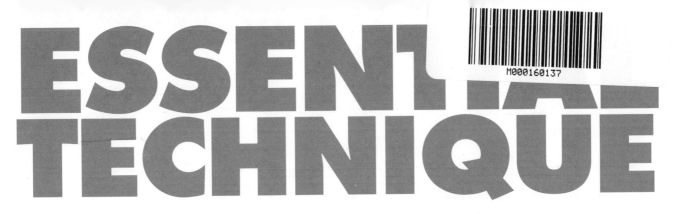

ESSENTIAL TECHNIQUE

Intermediate To Advanced Studies
Essential Elements Band Method

Tom C. Rhodes • Donald Bierschenk • Tim Lautzenheiser
John Higgins • Linda Petersen

WHY BAND?

Everyone loves music. From the awakening musical notes of the radio alarm to the final chord of your favorite television show's theme song, music is an important part of every day. Through melody and rhythm, music offers a level of communication that makes life itself more exciting and fulfilling.

Being in band gives you the opportunity to explore your own musical talents and skills while developing a life-long family of friends who share this artistic journey with you. You will discover a higher level of success in many parts of your life because of your experiences in band.

BAND IS MUSIC.
BAND IS FRIENDS.
BAND IS SELF-DISCIPLINE.
BAND IS PERFORMANCE.
BAND IS EXCITING.
BAND IS WORKING TOGETHER FOR A COMMON GOAL.
BAND IS A CHANCE TO EXPRESS YOUR TALENT.
BAND IS ENJOYMENT.
BAND IS HIGH ENERGY.
BAND IS YOU!

STRIKE UP THE BAND!

- Tim Lautzenheiser

ISBN 0-7935-1806-7

HAL•LEONARD™
CORPORATION
7777 W. BLUEMOUND RD. P.O. BOX 13819 MILWAUKEE, WI 53213

00863551

2

Concert Bb Major (Your G Major)

Ear training helps you blend in with the rest of the ensemble by teaching you to listen carefully. Tune each note on *Balance Builders,* starting with the lowest pitch.

1. BALANCE BUILDER

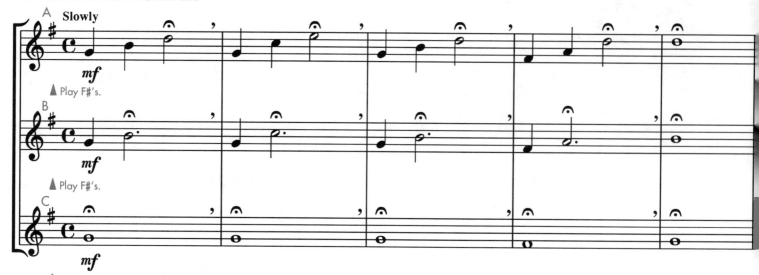

▲ Play F#'s.

2. CHORALE - Full Band Arrangement (Prelude from Hansel and Gretel)

Engelbert Humperdinck
Arr. John Higgins

Articulation Articulation is the way we tongue or slur notes. Staccato dots, tenuto marks and slurs tell us how to articulate each note. Notes without articulation marks should be tongued and played for full value. Articulations often occur in patterns, such as:

A.   B.   C.

3. CONCERT Bb MAJOR SCALE TECHNIQUE (Your G Major)

Practicing scales is the best way to improve your playing ability. Try them in various tempos, always keeping a steady pulse.

ARTICULATION WORK - OUT   Play even rhythms at all tempos.

CHILDREN'S SHOES

Black American Spiritual

Allegro

onducting   The two-beat conducting pattern is used for pieces written in $\frac{2}{4}$, ¢ or $\frac{2}{2}$, and fast $\frac{6}{8}$ meters. Practice conducting this two-beat pattern.

COME DOWN TO HILO

English Sea Song

Allegretto

Where is the "&" of beat 2? ▲

RESTS ALWAYS COUNT

Allegro

8. THE MOUNTAIN DEER CHASE

North American Folk Son[g]

Theory **Interval** The distance between two notes. Start with "1" on the lower note, and count each line and space between the notes. The number of the higher note tells us the name of the interval.

9. INTERVAL TECHNIQUE Write in the numbers of the intervals. Remember to count **up** from the lowest note.

Sightreading Playing a musical selection for the first time. The key to sightreading success is knowing what to look for before playing the piece. Follow the guidelines below, and your band will be sightreading STARS! Use the word **STARS** to remind yourself what to look for before reading a selection the first time.

S — **Sharps or flats** in the **key signature** Identify the key signature first. Silently practice notes from the key signature. Look for key signature changes in the piece.

T — **Time signature** and **tempo markings** Identify and look for changes in the piece.

A — **Accidentals** Check for any accidentals not found in the key signature.

R — **Rhythm** Slowly count and clap all difficult rhythms. Pay special attention to rests.

S — **Signs** Look for all signs that indicate dynamics, articulations, tempo changes, repeats, 1st and 2nd endings, and any other instructions printed on your music.

10. SIGHTREADING CHALLENGE #1

Puerto Rican Folk Son[g]

Where is beat 4? ▲

History German composer **Johann Sebastian Bach** (1685-1750) is the most famous composer of the Baroque era (1600-1750). Bach wrote many cantatas, which are long works for chorus, soloists and orchestra. "Sheep May Safely Graze" is from *Cantata 208,* written in 1713. European immigrants began to settle in the American colonies during Bach's lifetime.

Style Mark Indicates the manner or style in which the piece should be played. Style marks are usually found above the time signature.

1. SHEEP MAY SAFELY GRAZE - Duet
Johann Sebastian Bach

12. CHROMATIC TECHNIQUE

13. ESSENTIAL TECHNIQUE QUIZ - SPINNING SONG
Johann Ellmenreich

Ear Training — **Concert Eb Major (Your C Major)**   Singing is a common ear training exercise. Play each exercise below, then sing it in your natural voice range. Make sure you can hear all the notes when playing and singing.

14. BALANCE BUILDER

A **Slowly**

B ▲ Play all natural notes.

C ▲ Play all natural notes.

▲ Play all natural notes.

15. CHORALE - Full Band Arrangement
(Based on a Theme by Palestrina)

Arr. John Higgins

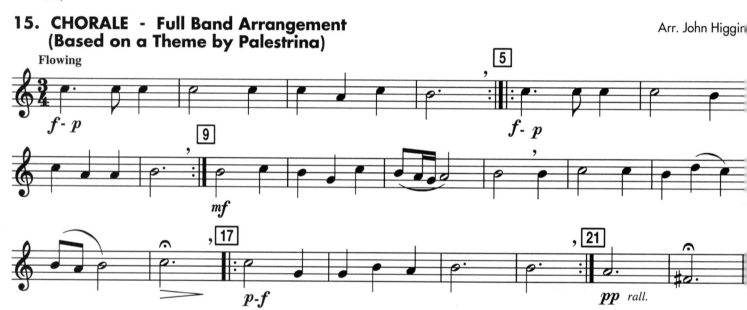

16. CONCERT Eb MAJOR TECHNIQUE (Your C Major)

Practice scales at all dynamic levels and in various tempos. Always keep a steady pulse.

Scale

Scale in Thirds

Arpeggio

17. ARTICULATION WORK - OUT   Play even rhythms at all tempos.

Conducting

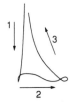

The three-beat pattern is used for pieces written in ¾, ⅜ and ⅝ meters. Practice conducting this three-beat pattern.

8. THE BIRTHDAY SONG

Allegro

f

Dynamics

pp (pianissimo) Play very softly.   *ff* (fortissimo) Play very loudly.

Always use full breath support to produce your best possible tone and intonation.

19. DYNAMIC CONTRASTS

Andante

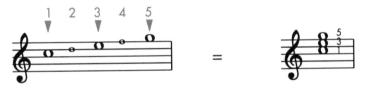

pp   p   mp   mf   f   ff   f   mf   mp   p   pp

Theory **Chords** Two or more different notes sounding simultaneously. Chords can be formed from scale steps. The most common chord is made up of the 1st, 3rd, and 5th scale steps. Here is a chord from the C Major scale:

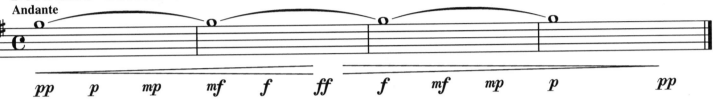

20. EAR TRAINING TECHNIQUE

Play each exercise below, then sing it in your natural voice range. Make sure you can hear all the notes of the chord in the last measure.

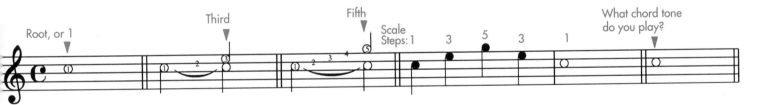

History Austrian composer **Johann Strauss Jr.** (1825-1899) is also known as "The Waltz King." He wrote some of the world's most famous waltzes (dances in 3/4 meter). This waltz is from *Die Fledermaus* ("The Bat"), Strauss' most famous operetta. Operettas were the forerunners of today's musicals, such as *Oklahoma, The Sound Of Music* and *The Phantom Of The Opera.*

21. ADELE'S SONG

Johann Strauss Jr.

Bright waltz tempo

22. O TANNENBAUM

German Carol

Moderato

23. RHYTHM RAP

24. KEEPIN' SECRETS

Appalachian Folk Song

Moderato

History American composer **Amy Marcy Beach** (1867-1944) was the first woman composer to have a major symphonic work (*Gaelic Symphony*, 1896) performed by the New York Philharmonic. She toured and performed in Europe after 1910, and was recognized as the first American woman composer to write works in the European style. Amy Marcy Beach, known at the time as Mrs. H. H. A. Beach, was a pioneer for today's women composers and performers.

25. SCOTTISH LEGEND

Amy Marcy Beach

Lento ◄ Very slow tempo

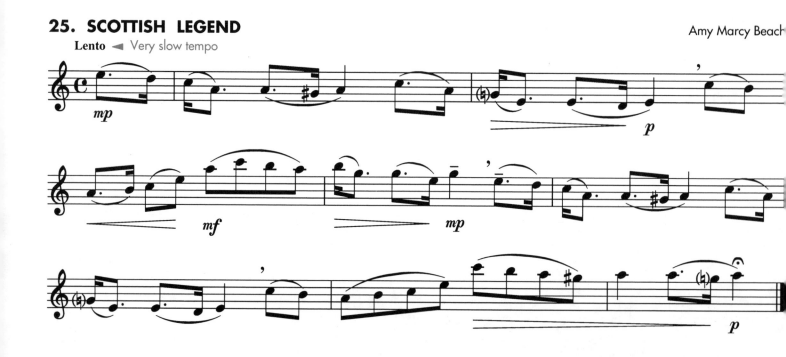

26. THE KEEL ROW
Sea Song

27. SMOOTH SAILING

Conducting

The four-beat pattern is used for pieces written in 4/4, 4/2 and 12/8 meters. Practice conducting this four-beat pattern.

28. CHROMATIC TECHNIQUE

C
Alternate fingering

Review the **STARS** guidelines before sightreading.

S — Sharps or flats in the key signature
T — Time signature and tempos
A — Accidentals
R — Rhythm
S — Signs

29. SIGHTREADING CHALLENGE #2 - COMIN' THROUGH THE RYE
Scottish Folk Song

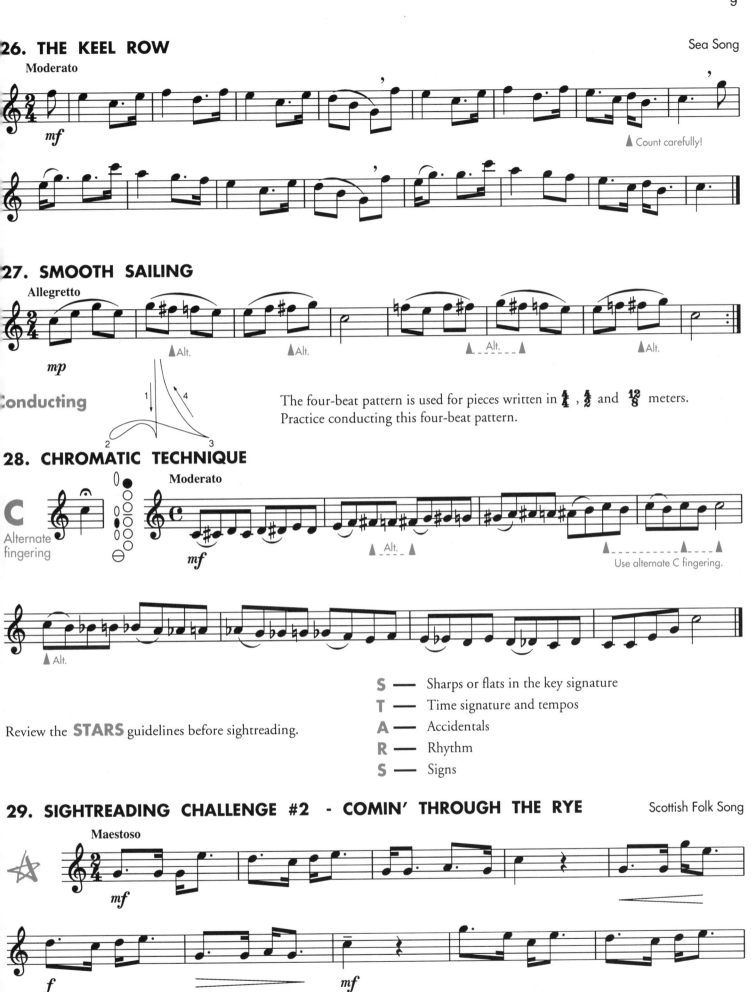

For centuries, **Native American Indian music** has been an important part of tribal dancing ceremonies. Apache fiddles, rattles, flutes and log drums accompanied simple songs. Much of today's Indian music has been influenced by Western and Afro-American cultures due to the forced migration of Indian tribes to reservations. American composer **Charles Wakefield Cadman** (1881-1946) wrote this song in 1914 based on Indian melodies he researched throughout his lifetime.

30. SONG OF THE WEEPING SPIRIT

Native American Indian Melody
Adapted by Charles Wakefield Cadman

Lento mysterioso ◄ Slowly and mysteriously

31. CELEBRATION SONG

Malaysian Wedding Song

Moderato

Key Signature Names

Key signature names tell us the "key" of the musical composition. The key is the tonal center, or "home base." A key signature without sharps or flats is usually called C Major. Identify the name of key signatures by remembering two simple rules:

1) **Flats look back.** The second-to-last flat tells us the key signature name.

For example, a key signature with 3 flats (Bb, Eb, Ab) is Eb Major:    A key signature with one flat is F Major:

2) **Sharps look up.** The note one half-step above the last sharp tells us the key signature name.

For example, a key signature with one sharp is G Major:

Here are some common key signatures:

F Major   Bb Major   Eb Major   C Major   G Major   D Major

32. ESSENTIAL TECHNIQUE QUIZ

Write the names of the following key signatures. The name of the whole note is the name of the key signature.

    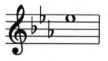 

Ear Training

Concert F Major (Your D Major)

Play each line below, then sing it in your natural voice range. Make sure all chord tones are heard equally well and are in "balance." Begin tuning with the lower instruments of the band.

3. BALANCE BUILDER

4. CHORALE - Full Band Arrangement (Based on a Theme by J. S. Bach)

Arr. John Higgins

35. CONCERT F MAJOR TECHNIQUE (Your D Major)

36. ARTICULATION WORK - OUT Play even rhythms at all tempos.

37. RHYTHM RAP

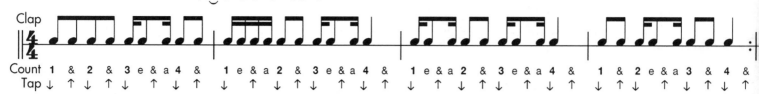

38. CONCERT F MAJOR SCALE (Your D Major)

Moderato

History French composer **Claude Debussy** (1862-1918) created moods and "impressions" with his music. While earlier composers used music to describe events (such as Tchaikovsky's *1812 Overture*), Debussy's new ideas helped shape today's music. The style of art and music created in this time is called "impressionism." The first automobile was produced during Debussy's lifetime. He died the same year that World War I ended.

39. THE LITTLE CHILD

Claude Debussy

Giocoso ◄ Lightly, happily

40. TURKEY IN THE STRAW

American Folk Song

Allegretto

44. THAT'S A PLENTY

Lew Pollack

45. CHROMATIC TECHNIQUE

Jazz is a uniquely American art form, and continues to influence today's popular music. It developed in the 20th century when black musicians began combining African and European musical styles. "Dixieland" was a popular early jazz form, and the first jazz recording was made during World War I by the Original Dixieland Band in New Orleans. *That's A Plenty* is a famous Dixieland song.

14

History Composers often use traditional folk songs within their music. Band composer John Barnes Chance used this simple tune in his *Variations On A Korean Folk Song*, now a famous work for concert band. The melody uses only the 1st, 2nd, 3rd, 5th and 6th notes from the Concert B♭ major scale. This type of scale is called a pentatonic scale. "Penta" is the Latin word for "five."

46. KOREAN FOLK SONG THEME

Korean Folk Song

Divisi Tells players to "divide" and play the two (or more) notes written on the same staff. Be sure to decide who plays upper and lower notes before playing the piece. *Divisi* is usually abbreviated *div.* *Unis.*, or unison, tells performers to play the same note.

47. MINUET   E-sharp is played with the same fingering as F-natural.

Ludwig van Beethoven

Marcato Accent ∧   A loud accented note of short duration.

48. ESSENTIAL TECHNIQUE QUIZ - RHYTHM CHALLENGE

Sixteenth Rest

𝄿 = 1/4 silent beat

𝄿	= 1/4 silent beat
𝄾	= 1/2 silent beat
𝄽	= 1 silent beat

𝄿 𝄿 𝄿 𝄿 𝄿 𝄿 𝄿 𝄿

1 e & a **2** e & a

↓   ↑   ↓   ↑

A sixteenth rest has two flags on the stem.

▼ Flags

𝄿

49. RHYTHM RAP

Clap

Count **1** & **2** e & a | **1** e & a **2** & | **1** e & a **2** & | **1** e & a **2** &

Tap ↓ ↑ ↓ ↑ | ↓ ↑ ↓ ↑ | ↓ ↑ ↓ ↑ | ↓ ↑ ↓ ↑

50. COUNT CAREFULLY

Moderato

mf

51. ARTICULATION WORK - OUT

f

52. CHROMATIC TECHNIQUE

Use alternate C fingering.

▲ Alt.

53. FRENCH NATIONAL ANTHEM (LA MARSEILLAISE)

Rouget De L'Isle

Allegro marziale ◄ March-like style

1 & **2** & **3** e & a

f

16

After 1755, a group of French-speaking Canadians living in what is now Nova Scotia migrated to southern Louisiana, calling themselves "Acadians." Their music is called **Cajun music**, and remains a significant part of American culture. Today's Cajun bands are usually made up of a fiddle, accordion, electric guitar, bass and drum set. The first Cajun recording was made in 1928, one year after the first television transmission.

54. ACADIAN DANCE

Sixteenth Notes in 6/8

55. RHYTHM RAP

56. ARTICULATION WORK - OUT

57. RHYTHM RAP

58. THE DOT ALWAYS COUNTS HALF

Conducting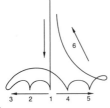

The six-beat pattern is used for pieces written in **6/8** meter. **6/8** pieces can also be conducted with a two-beat pattern, emphasizing beats 1 and 4. Practice conducting this six-beat pattern.

59. SONATA

Wolfgang Amadeus Mozart

Andante grazioso ◄ Gracefully

60. ARPEGGIO EXTENSION

E

Moderato

 Music written during the Renaissance era (1430-1600) was often upbeat and dance-like. *Wolsey's Wilde* was originally written for the lute, an ancestor to the guitar and the most popular instrument of the Renaissance era. Modern day concert band composer Gordon Jacob used this popular song in his *William Byrd Suite*, written as a tribute to English composer William Byrd (1543-1623).

61. WOLSEY'S WILDE

Anonymous

Animato ◄ Animated, lively

 **Minor Scales**   A **Minor Scale** is a series of eight notes which follow a definite pattern of whole steps and half steps. The three forms of the minor scale are natural minor, harmonic minor and melodic minor.

62. NATURAL MINOR - Follows the key signature. Half steps appear only between scale steps 2-3 and 5-6.

63. HARMONIC MINOR - Like natural minor, except the 7th scale step is raised one-half step.

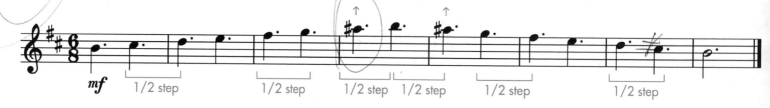

64. MELODIC MINOR

    Ascending - Like natural minor, except the 6th and 7th scale steps are raised one-half step.
    Descending - Just like natural minor.

65. CHORALE - Full Band Arrangement
(Based on a Theme by Tchaikovsky)

Arr. John Higgins

66. CONCERT D MELODIC MINOR TECHNIQUE   (Your B Melodic Minor)

Minor Chords Here is a chord from the B Minor scale. It is made up of the 1st, 3rd and 5th scale steps.

67. EAR TRAINING TECHNIQUE Play each exercise below, then sing it in your natural voice range.
Make sure you can hear all the notes of the chord in the last measure.

68. GREENSLEEVES English Folk Song

69. INTERVAL TECHNIQUE

S	—	Sharps or flats in the key signature
T	—	Time signature and tempos
A	—	Accidentals
R	—	Rhythm
S	—	Signs

Review the **STARS** guidelines before sightreading.

70. SIGHTREADING CHALLENGE #3 - TARANTELLA

20

Ear Training — Concert A♭ Major (Your F Major)

Play each line below, then sing it in your natural voice range. Make sure all chord tones are heard equally well and are in "balance." Begin tuning with lower instruments of the band.

71. BALANCE BUILDER

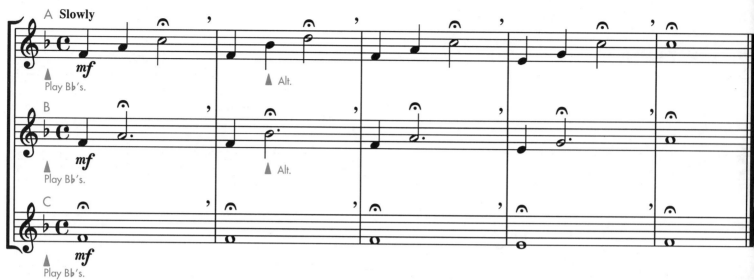

72. CHORALE - Full Band Arrangement (Erhalt Uns In Der Wahrheit)

Johann Sebastian Bach
Arr. John Higgins

73. CONCERT A♭ MAJOR SCALE TECHNIQUE (Your F Major)

74. ARTICULATION WORK - OUT   Play even rhythms at all tempos.

The Star Spangled Banner is the national anthem of the United States of America. Francis Scott Key wrote the words during the 1814 battle at Fort McHenry. He listened to the sounds of the fighting throughout the night while being detained on a ship. At dawn, he saw the American flag still flying over the fort. He was inspired to write these words, which were later set to the melody of a popular English song.

Words by Francis Scott Key
Music by John Stafford Smith

75. THE STAR SPANGLED BANNER

SPECIAL WOODWIND EXERCISES

Trill *tr*   Rapidly alternate between a note and the note above (or below). *tr* and *tr*⌢⌢⌢ are common trill abbreviations. Always trill to the note above the written note (in the key signature) unless the music indicates another trill note. You may need to use alternate fingerings when playing trills. Move the trill key (or keys) as quickly as possible. Trills should be played smoothly.

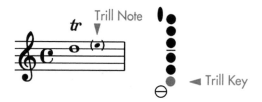

WHOLE STEP TRILLS   Practice these trills with the indicated fingerings:

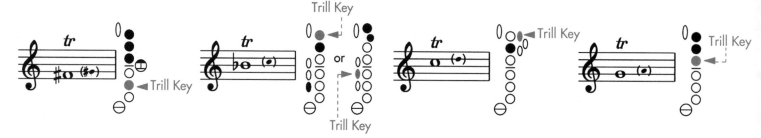

HALF STEP TRILLS

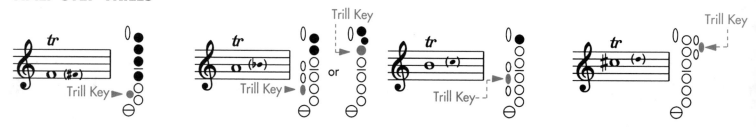

History   Italian composer **Antonio Vivaldi** (1678-1741) lived during the Baroque era (1600-1750). Vivaldi completed *The Four Seasons* in 1726, just a few years before Benjamin Franklin discovered electricity. *The Four Seasons* was written to describe autumn, winter, spring and summer. This is the theme from the first movement, "Spring."

78. THEME FROM THE FOUR SEASONS

Antonio Vivaldi

Concert C Major (Your A Major)

Concert C Major challenges players to listen and tune very carefully. After warming up, you may need to adjust your instrument and/or embouchure to play all notes in tune. Play each line below, then sing it in your natural voice range. Make sure all chord tones are heard equally well and are in "balance."

79. BALANCE BUILDER

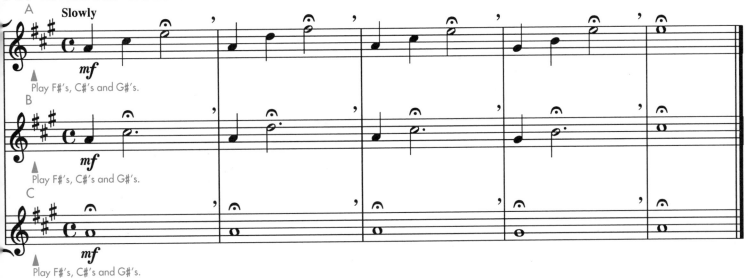

80. CHORALE - Full Band Arrangement (Navy Hymn)

John Dykes
Arr. John Higgins

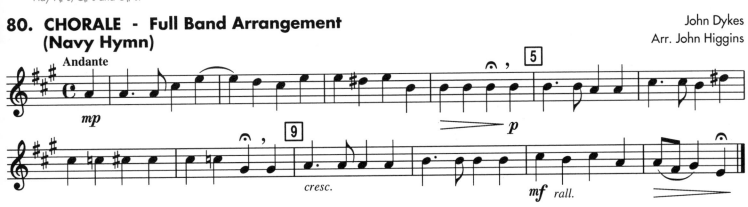

81. CONCERT C MAJOR TECHNIQUE (Your A Major)

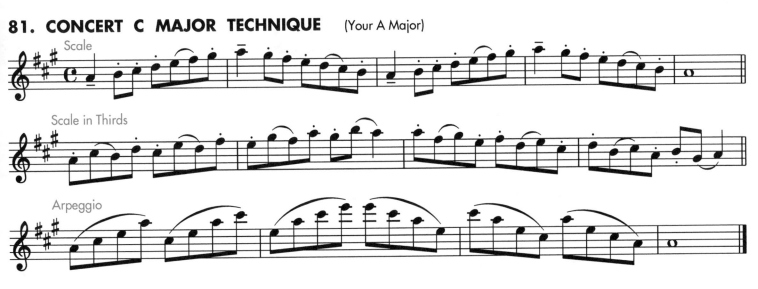

82. ARTICULATION WORK - OUT   Play even rhythms at all tempos.

83. CHILD OF THE RAINBOW

Chinese Folk Song

Andante

f ◄ Follow the dynamics carefully.

Black American spirituals originated in the 1700's. As one of the largest categories of true American folk music, these melodies were sung and passed on for generations without being written down. Black and white people worked together to publish the first spiritual collection in 1867, four years after The Emancipation Proclamation was signed into law.

84. SIT DOWN, SISTER

Black American Spiritual

Allegro

85. ESSENTIAL TECHNIQUE QUIZ - METER MANIA #1

Happily

Concert G Minor (Your E Minor) Compare the sound of these minor chords with the major chords found in other *Balance Builders.* Which chord tone creates the unique sound of a minor chord?

86. BALANCE BUILDER

87. CHORALE - Full Band Arrangement (Prelude)

Frederic Chopin
Arr. John Higgins

Adagio

88. CONCERT G MELODIC MINOR TECHNIQUE (Your E Melodic Minor)

89. ARTICULATION WORK - OUT   Play even rhythms at all tempos.

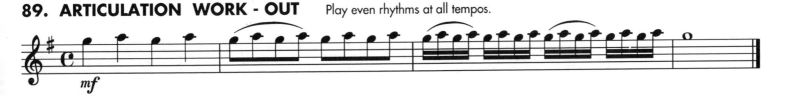

Native Japanese instruments include the *shakuhachi*, a bamboo flute played pointing downward; the *koto*, a long zither with movable frets played sitting down; and the *gakubiwa*, a pear-shaped lute with strings that are plucked. These instruments have been an important part of Japanese culture since the 8th century. *Kabuki*, a Japanese theatrical form that originated in 1603, remains popular in Japan. Performers play native Japanese instruments during Kabuki performances.

90. SONG OF THE SHAKUHACHI

Japanese Folk Son

91. CONCERT B♭ SCALE IN FOURTHS

Important French composers of the late 19th century include **Claude Debussy** (1862-1918), **Gabriel Fauré** (1845-1924), **Erik Satie** (1866-1925), **César Franck** (1822-1890), **Camille Saint-Saëns** (1835-1921) and **Paul Dukas** (1865-1935). Their works continue to have influence on the music of modern day composers. Gabriel Fauré wrote *Pavanne* (originally for orchestra) in 1887, two years before the Eiffel Tower was completed in Paris.

92. PAVANNE

Gabriel Fauré

Enharmonics

Notes that have different note names, but sound the same and are played with the same fingering. Enharmonics often appear in chromatic patterns. Alternate fingerings make it easier to play certain chromatic passages. Practice this exercise slowly, and carefully follow the indicated fingerings. Be sure to use alternate fingerings when these chromatic patterns appear in your band music.

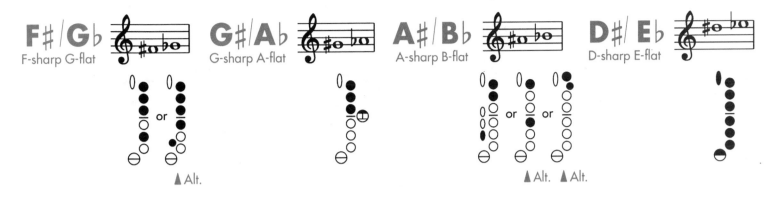

F♯/G♭ F-sharp G-flat   **G♯/A♭** G-sharp A-flat   **A♯/B♭** A-sharp B-flat   **D♯/E♭** D-sharp E-flat

93. CHROMATIC TECHNIQUE

Moderato

Time Signature (Meter)

3 - 3 beats per measure
8 - ♪ or 𝄾 gets one beat

There are two ways to count ⅜ meter:

3 beats to a measure with the eighth note receiving one beat.   **OR**   1 beat to a measure with 3 eighth notes (or the equivalent) receiving one beat.

94. RHYTHM RAP

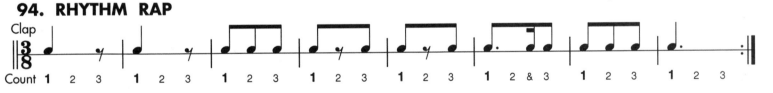

Clap   Count 1 2 3 | 1 2 3 | 1 2 3 | 1 2 3 | 1 2 3 | 1 2 & 3 | 1 2 3 | 1 2 3

95. THE SORCERER'S APPRENTICE

Paul Dukas

Allegro agitato ◄ Agitated

96. BLOW, YE WINDS, WESTERLY

English Sea Song

Where is beat 3?

97. SANTA LUCIA

Teodore Cottrau

98. ESSENTIAL TECHNIQUE QUIZ

Knowing the names of the sharps and flats is a very important part of learning to read key signatures. The names of several common key signatures are listed below. Write the name of the sharps or flats on the line labeled "Play."

Bb Major/G minor
Play Bb's and Eb's

F Major/D minor
Play_____

Eb Major/C minor
Play _____

Ab Major/F minor
Play _____

C Major/A minor
Play _____

G Major/E minor
Play_____

D Major/B minor
Play _____

A Major/F# minor
Play _____

Grace Note ♪ A small note (or notes) which is played on or slightly before the beat.

99. JULIET'S WALTZ
Charles Gounod

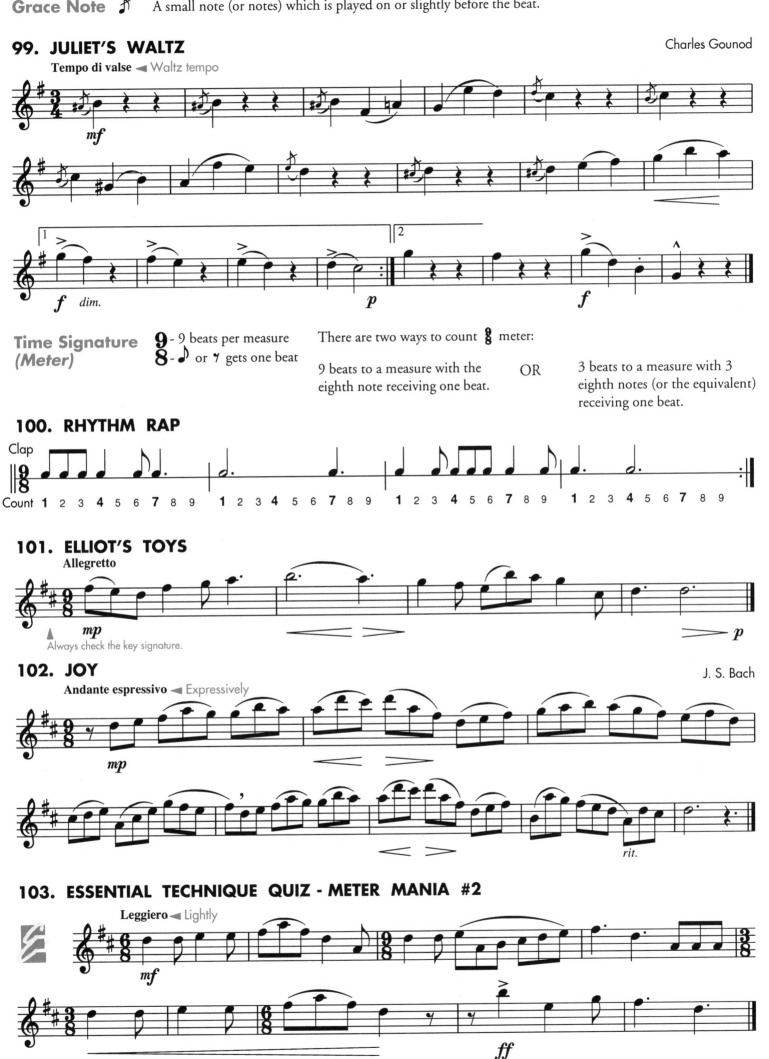

Tempo di valse ◄ Waltz tempo

Time Signature (Meter)
9 - 9 beats per measure
8 - ♪ or 𝄾 gets one beat

There are two ways to count **9/8** meter:

9 beats to a measure with the eighth note receiving one beat.

OR

3 beats to a measure with 3 eighth notes (or the equivalent) receiving one beat.

100. RHYTHM RAP

Clap

Count **1** 2 3 **4** 5 6 **7** 8 9   **1** 2 3 **4** 5 6 **7** 8 9   **1** 2 3 **4** 5 6 **7** 8 9   **1** 2 3 **4** 5 6 **7** 8 9

101. ELLIOT'S TOYS
Allegretto

▲ Always check the key signature.

102. JOY
J. S. Bach

Andante espressivo ◄ Expressively

rit.

103. ESSENTIAL TECHNIQUE QUIZ - METER MANIA #2

Leggiero ◄ Lightly

Transposing Instruments

A note name is part of the complete name of many instruments, such as F Horn, Bb Clarinet and Eb Alto Saxophone. This note name is the actual sounding pitch heard when a written "C" is played on the instrument. The chart below tells you the actual sounding pitches heard when these common band instruments play a written "C."

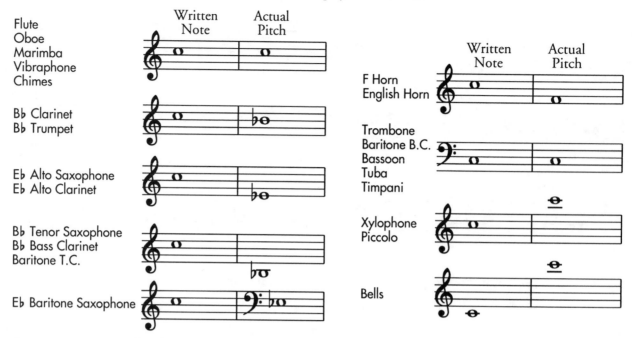

As you can see, many band instruments **sound lower** than their written pitches. Composers and arrangers must think of the actual note they want each instrument to play, and adjust the written note so it matches the intended pitch. This process is called **transposition.**

Transposing instruments allow woodwind players to use the same fingerings when playing instruments in the same family. For example, clarinet fingerings are virtually the same on all types of clarinets. Treble clef brass instrument transposition is based on the harmonic series where "C" is played with open valves. The actual sounding pitch is a Bb for trumpets and an F for horns.

104. WHAT'S YOUR PITCH?

Find the name of your instrument on the chart above. Write the actual sounding pitch of your instrument when you play this written "C":

What is the name of this note? _____

105. TRUMPET TUNE

Henry Purcell

History Russian composers **Alexander Borodin** (1833-1887), **Modest Mussorgsky** (1839-1881), and **Nicolas Rimsky-Korsakov** (1844-1908) used native folk songs in their music. Their work inspired the next generation of Russian writers, including **Sergei Prokofiev** (1891-1953) and **Mikhail Ippolitov-Ivanov** (1859-1935). Prokofiev's *March From The Love Of Three Oranges* and Ippolitov-Ivanov's *The Sadar's Procession* were both written around the same time as the Wright brothers' first successful airplane flight.

106. MARCH FROM THE LOVE OF THREE ORANGES
Sergei Prokofiev

107. THE SADAR'S PROCESSION
Mikhail Ippolitov-Ivanov

108. CORONATION MARCH
Giacomo Meyerbeer

Quarter Note Triplet = 2 beats

Quarter note triplet is 3 notes that equal 2 beats.

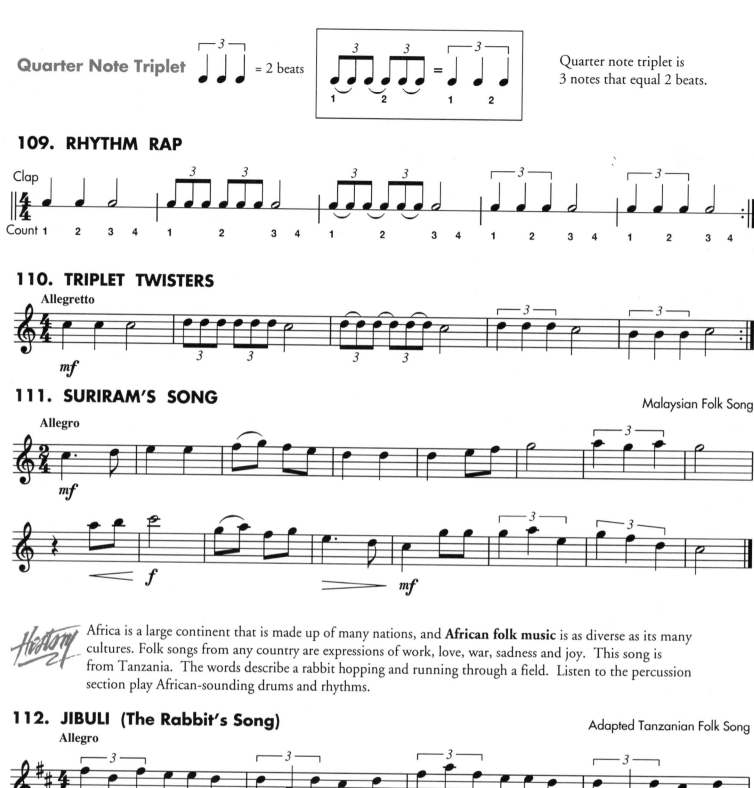

109. RHYTHM RAP

110. TRIPLET TWISTERS

111. SURIRAM'S SONG

Malaysian Folk Song

History — Africa is a large continent that is made up of many nations, and **African folk music** is as diverse as its many cultures. Folk songs from any country are expressions of work, love, war, sadness and joy. This song is from Tanzania. The words describe a rabbit hopping and running through a field. Listen to the percussion section play African-sounding drums and rhythms.

112. JIBULI (The Rabbit's Song)

Adapted Tanzanian Folk Song

Time Signature (Meter) $\frac{12}{8}$ — 12 beats per measure
$\frac{}{8}$ — ♪ or 𝄾 gets one beat

There are two ways to count $\frac{12}{8}$ meter:

12 beats to a measure with the eighth note receiving one beat.

OR

4 beats to a measure with 3 eighth notes (or the equivalent) receiving one beat.

113. RHYTHM RAP

Clap

Count **1** 2 3 **4** 5 6 **7** 8 9 **10** 11 12 | **1** 2 3 **4** 5 6 **7** 8 9 **10** 11 12 | **1** 2 3 **4** 5 6 **7** 8 9 **10** 11 12

114. COUNT TO TWELVE

Andante

mp

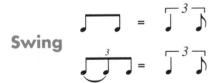

African-American composer **W. C. Handy** (1873-1958), the "Father of the Blues", was the first to publish popular blues songs. "Blues" is a term which describes scale notes and a style of music. Scale notes are altered (or "bent") to create "blue" notes. The blues style is a 12-bar chord progression that serves as the basis for improvisation. *St. Louis Blues* was written in 1914, the same year that World War I began. Blues artists include singers Ma Rainey and Bessie Smith, and instrumental performers Muddy Waters and B. B. King.

115. ST. LOUIS BLUES

W.C. Handy

Moderate blues tempo

mf

Swing

Swing eighth notes are played with an uneven division of the beat. When the style mark indicates "swing", play eighth notes as if they were written: Swing notation denotes a popular style often used in jazz music.

116. ST. LOUIS BLUES SWING

W.C. Handy

Moderate swing

mf

Time Signature (Meter)

$\mathbf{3}$ - 3 beats per measure
$\mathbf{2}$ - 𝅗𝅥 or ▬ gets one beat

Use the three-beat conducting pattern for $\frac{3}{2}$ pieces.

117. RHYTHM RAP

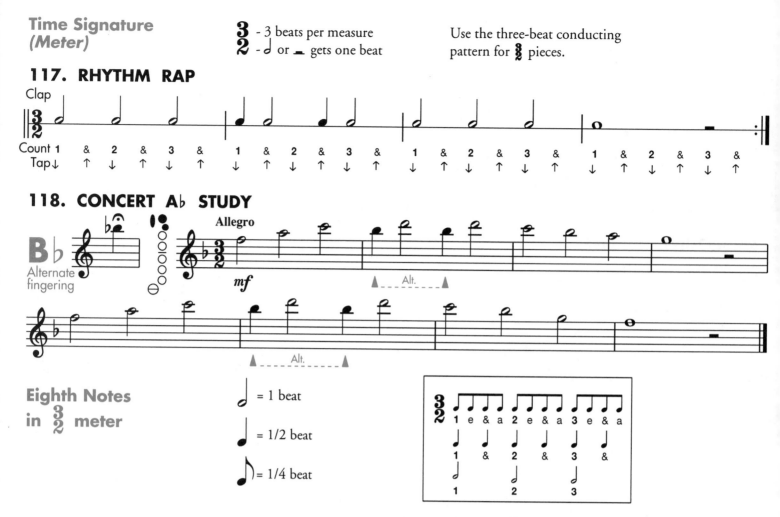

118. CONCERT A♭ STUDY

B♭
Alternate fingering

Eighth Notes in $\frac{3}{2}$ meter

𝅗𝅥 = 1 beat

𝅘𝅥 = 1/2 beat

𝅘𝅥𝅮 = 1/4 beat

English composer **George Frideric Handel** (1685-1759) lived during the Baroque era (1600-1750). *Water Music* was written in honor of England's King George I. The first performance took place on the Thames River on July 17, 1717. Fifty musicians performed the work while floating on a barge. Handel lived during the same time as Johann Sebastian Bach, perhaps the most famous Baroque composer.

119. WATER MUSIC

George Frideric Handel

Time Signature (Meter) **5** - 5 beats per measure **4** - ♩ or 𝄽 gets one beat

Conducting

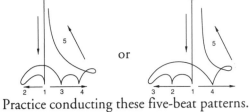

Practice conducting these five-beat patterns.

120. RHYTHM RAP

121. CONCERT A♭ REVIEW

122. SUKURU ITO

African Folk Song

Where is beat 5?

123. CHROMATIC TECHNIQUE

124. ESSENTIAL TECHNIQUE QUIZ - PICTURES AT AN EXHIBITION

Modest Mussorgsky

Concert G Major
(Your E Major)

Play each exercise below, then sing it in your natural voice range. Make sure all chord tones are heard equally well and are in "balance." Begin tuning with the lower instruments of the band.

125. BALANCE BUILDER

A

Slowly

mf

Play F#'s, C#'s, G#'s and D#'s.

B

mf

Play F#'s, C#'s, G#'s and D#'s.

C

mf

Play F#'s, C#'s, G#'s and D#'s.

126. CHORALE - Full Band Arrangement
(All Beautiful The March Of Days)

Ralph Vaughan Williams
Arr. John Higgins

Adagio

mp

9

< *mf*

> *mp*

rit.

127. CONCERT G MAJOR TECHNIQUE   (Your E Major)

Scale

Scale in Thirds

Arpeggio

128. ARTICULATION WORK - OUT   Play even rhythms at all tempos.

mf

129. ENGLISH CHORALE - Duet

Franz Josef Haydn

Norwegian composer **Edvard Grieg** (1843-1907) based much of his music on the folk songs and dances of Norway. During the late 19th century, composers often used melodies from their native land. This trend is called **nationalism.** Russian **Modest Mussorgsky** (1839-1881), Czech **Antonin Dvořák** (1841-1904) and Englishman **Sir Edward Elgar** (1857-1934) are other famous composers whose music was influenced by nationalism.

130. NORWEGIAN DANCE

Edvard Grieg

Several twentieth century composers began to expand the traditional rules of music and harmony. **Arnold Schoenberg** (1874-1951) was the first composer to use a fixed sequence of twelve pitches. This technique is known as **serialism.** **Alban Berg** (1885-1935), **Igor Stravinsky** (1882-1971) and **Anton Webern** (1883-1945) also used serialism in their music. *Twelve Tones* is an example of this type of music. This melody does not have a key center, and includes some "dissonant" interval distances between notes.

131. TWELVE TONES

Ear Training | **Concert D Major (Your B Major)** | Play each exercise below, then sing it in your natural voice range. Make sure all chord tones are heard equally well and are in "balance." Begin tuning with the lower instruments of the band.

132. BALANCE BUILDER

Play F#'s, C#'s, G#'s, D#'s and A#'s.

133. CHORALE - Full Band Arrangement
(With One Voice)

John Higgins

134. CONCERT D MAJOR TECHNIQUE (Your B Major)

135. ARTICULATION WORK - OUT Play even rhythms at all tempos.

▲ Use alternate A# fingering on all A#'s.

136. BOUND FOR SOUTH AUSTRALIA
Australian Folk Song

137. EAR TRAINING TECHNIQUE
Play each exercise below, then sing it in your natural voice range.
Make sure you can hear all the notes of the chord in the last measure.

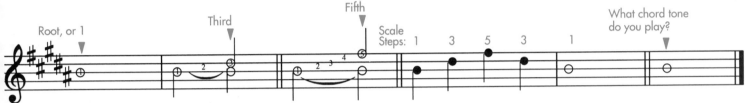

138. INTERVAL TECHNIQUE

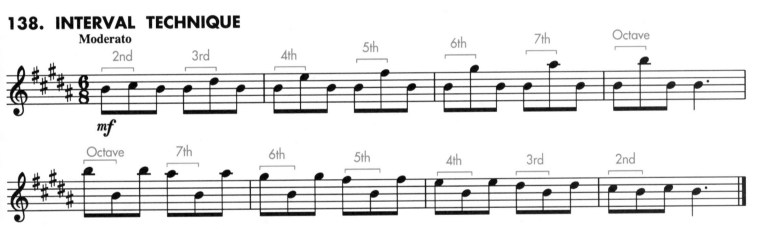

Latin American music combines the folk music from South and Central America, the Caribbean Islands, American Indian, Spanish and Portuguese cultures. Melodies are often accompanied by drums, maracas and claves. Latin American music continues to influence jazz, classical and popular styles of music. *Cielito Lindo* is a Latin American love song.

139. CIELITO LINDO
C. Fernandez

Concert Db Major (Your Bb Major) Play each exercise below, then sing it in your natural voice range. Make sure all chord tones are heard equally well and are in "balance." Begin tuning with the lower instruments of the band.

140. BALANCE BUILDER

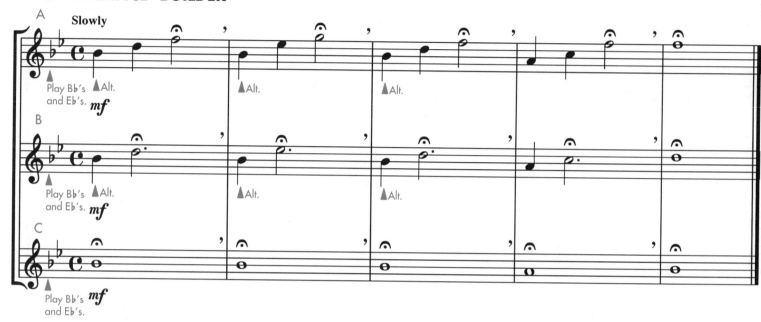

141. CONCERT Db MAJOR TECHNIQUE   (Your Bb Major)

142. GERMAN NATIONAL ANTHEM

Franz Josef Haydn

Concert Gb Major
(Your Eb Major)

Play each exercise below, then sing it in your natural voice range. Make sure all chord tones are heard equally well and are in "balance." Begin tuning with the lower instruments of the band.

143. BALANCE BUILDER

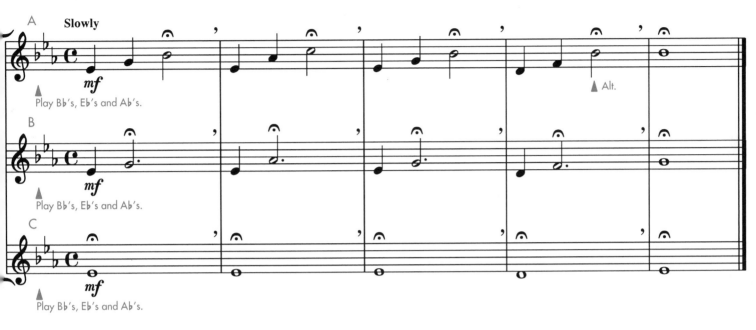

144. CONCERT Gb MAJOR TECHNIQUE   (Your Eb Major)

145. SPRING SONG

Felix Mendelssohn

Major Scales

Play major scales as part of your daily practice routine. Play all octaves, keys and arpeggios at various dynamic levels and tempos. Keep a steady pulse. Try different articulation patterns, such as:

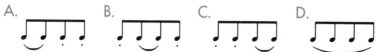

146. CONCERT B♭ MAJOR SCALE (Your G Major)

147. CONCERT E♭ MAJOR SCALE (Your C Major)

148. CONCERT F MAJOR SCALE (Your D Major)

149. CONCERT C MAJOR SCALE (Your A Major)

150. CONCERT A♭ MAJOR SCALE (Your F Major)

151. CONCERT Db MAJOR SCALE (Your Bb Major)

▼ Use alternate Bb fingering for all Bb's in this line.

152. CONCERT G MAJOR SCALE (Your E Scale)

153. CONCERT D MAJOR SCALE (Your B Major)

154. CONCERT A MAJOR SCALE (Your F# Major)

▲ Use alternate A# fingering for all A#'s in this line.

155. CONCERT Gb MAJOR SCALE (Your Eb Major)

▼ Use alternate Bb fingering for all Bb's in this line.

44

Minor Scales Play minor scales as part of your daily practice routine. Play all octaves, all three forms and the arpeggios at various dynamic levels and tempos. Keep a steady pulse. Try different articulation patterns, such as:

156. CONCERT D MINOR SCALE (Your B Minor)

157. CONCERT G MINOR SCALE (Your E Minor)

158. CONCERT C MINOR SCALE (Your A Minor)

159. CONCERT F MINOR SCALE (Your D Minor)

E♭ ALTO SAXOPHONE TRILL CHART

Here are some common trill fingerings. Trill key(s) appear in color.

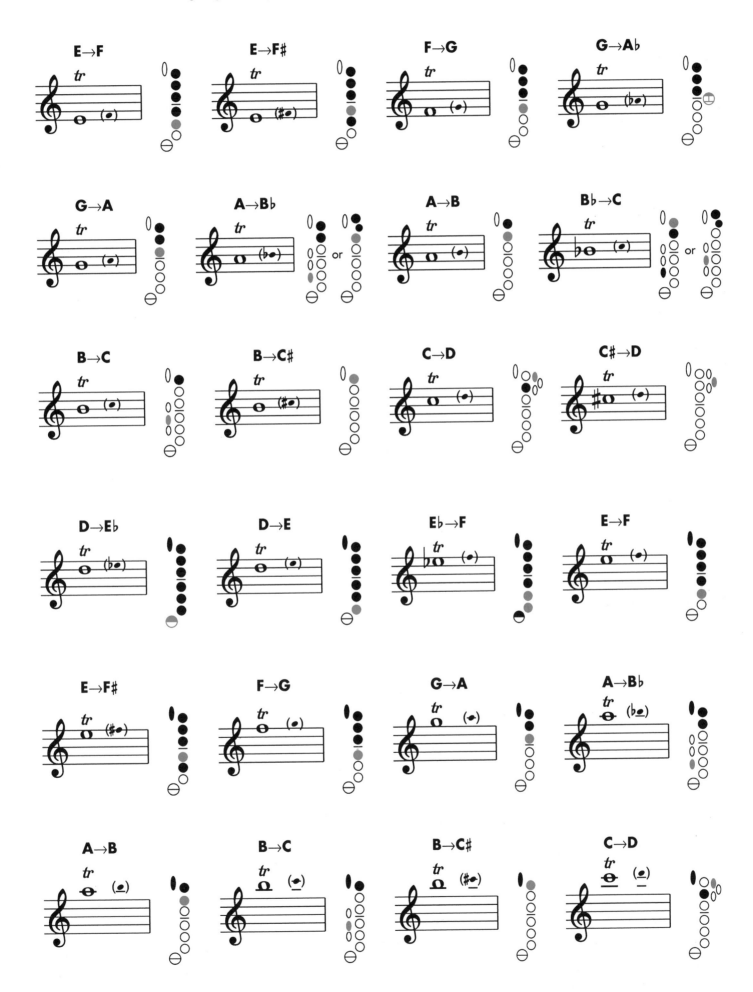

E♭ ALTO SAXOPHONE FINGERING CHART

Take Special Care

Before putting your instrument back in its case after playing, do the following:

- Remove the reed and wipe off excess moisture. Return to reed case.
- Remove mouthpiece and wipe the inside with a clean cloth. Wash your mouthpiece once per week with warm tap water. Dry thoroughly.
- Remove the neck and shake out excess moisture. Dry with neck cleaner.
- Drop the weight of the chamois or cotton swab into the bell. Pull the swab through the body several times. Return the instrument to its case.

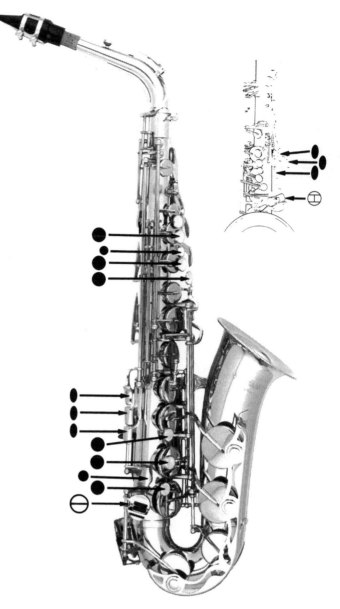

 = OPEN

● = PRESSED DOWN

The most common fingering appears first when two fingerings are shown.

Instrument courtesy of
Yamaha Corporation of America
Band and Orchestral Division.

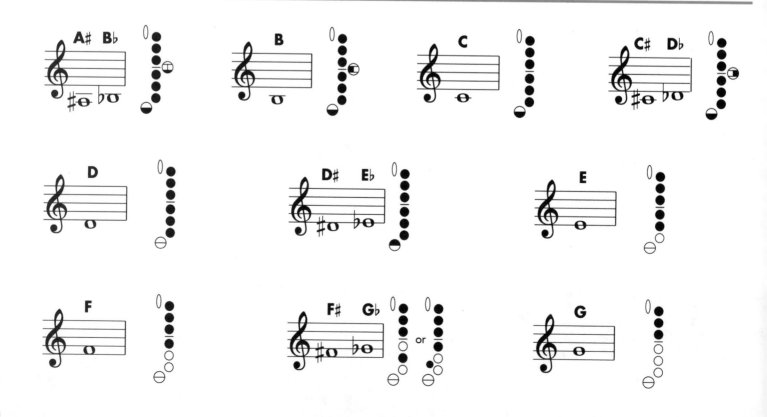

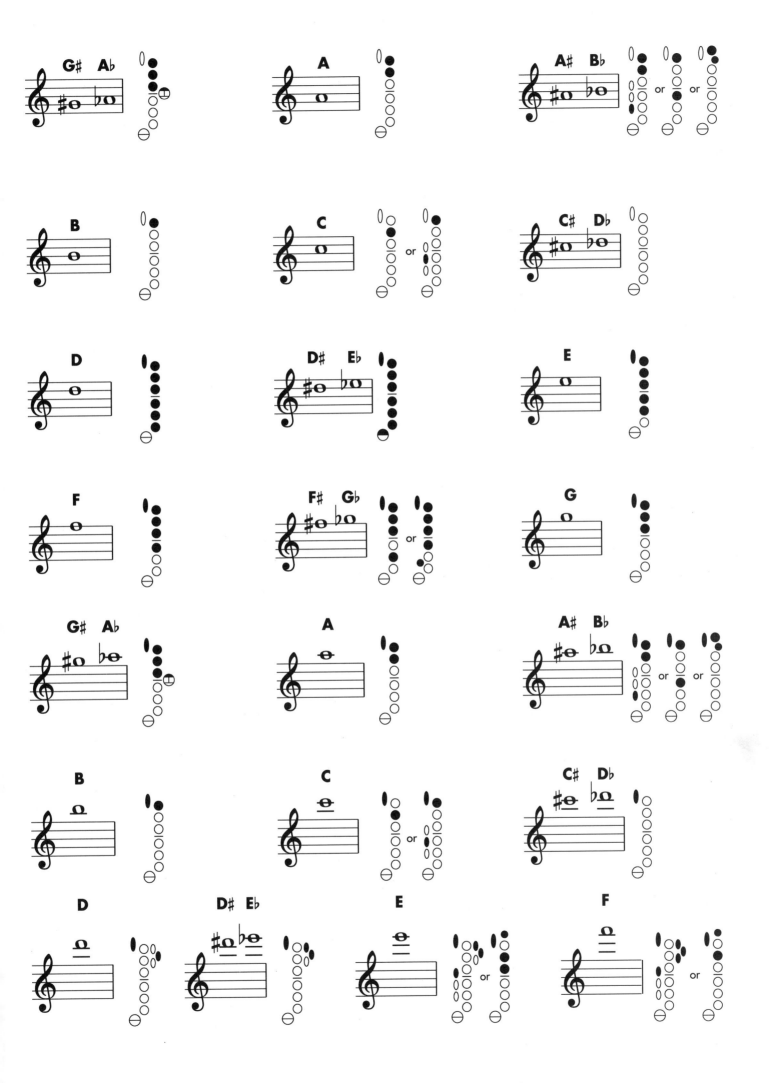

GLOSSARY

Essential Element	Definition	Essential Element	Definition
Accelerando *accel.*	Gradually increase the tempo.	Leggiero	Lightly.
Accent	Emphasize the note.	Lento	Very slow tempo.
Accidentals	Sharps, flats, and naturals found in the music.	Maestoso	Play in a majestic, stately manner.
		Major Scale	Series of 8 notes with a definite pattern of whole steps and half steps.
Adagio	Slow tempo, slower than Andante.		
Agitato	Agitated.	Marcato Accent	A loud accented note of short duration.
Allegretto	A lively tempo.		
Allegro	Fast, bright tempo.	Marziale	March-like style.
Andante	Slow walking tempo.	Measure Repeat	Repeat the previous measure.
Animato	Animated, lively.	Melodic Minor Scale	Like the natural minor, except the 6th
Arpeggio	A sequence of notes from any scale.		and 7th scale steps are raised by
Articulation	The way we tongue or slur notes.		one half-step when the scale is
Balance	The proper adjustment of volume from all instruments.		ascending. Same as natural minor when descending.
Bass Clef	"F" clef used by trombone, baritone, bassoon, and tuba.	*mezzo forte* **mf**	Play moderately loud.
		mezzo piano **mp**	Play moderately soft.
Chord	Two or more notes sounding simultaneously.	Minor Chord	Made up of the 1st, 3rd, and 5th scale steps of a minor scale.
Chromatic Scale	Sequence of notes in half-steps.	Minor Scale	Series of 8 notes with a definite pattern of whole steps and half-steps.
Chromatics	Notes that are altered with sharps, flats and naturals.		
		Moderato	Moderate tempo.
Common Time **C**	Another way to write $\frac{4}{4}$.	Mysterioso	Mysteriously.
Crescendo	Gradually increase volume.	Natural Minor Scale	Minor scale with half-steps between scale steps 2-3 and 5-6.
Cut Time **¢**	Meter in which the half note gets one beat.		
		Natural Sign ♮	Cancels a flat ♭ or sharp ♯ in the measure.
D.C. al Fine	*Da Capo al Fine* - Play until *D.C. al Fine*. Go back to the beginning and play until *Fine*.		
		Pentatonic Scale	Five note scale.
		pianissimo **pp**	Play very softly.
D.S. al Fine	*Del Segno al Fine* - Play until *D.S. al Fine*. Go back to the sign (𝄋) and play until *Fine*.	*piano* **p**	Play softly.
		Pick-up Notes	Notes that come before the first full measure.
Decrescendo	Gradually decrease volume.	Rallentando *rall.*	Gradually slow the tempo.
Divisi *div.*	Divide the notes between players.	Repeat Sign	Go back to the beginning and play again.
Dixieland	A popular form of early jazz.		
Dolce	Sweet, gentle style.		Repeat the section of music enclosed by the repeat signs.
Double Bar	Indicates the end of a piece of music.		
Dynamics	The volume of music.	Ritardando *rit.*	Gradually slow the tempo.
Enharmonics	Notes that are written differently but sound the same.	Sharp ♯	Raises the note and remains in effect the entire measure.
Espressivo	Expressivly.	Sightreading	Playing a musical selection for the first time.
Fermata	Hold the note longer, or until your director tells you to release it.		
		Simile *sim.*	Continue in the same style.
1st and 2nd Endings	Play the first ending the first time through. Then repeat the same music, skip the first ending and play the 2nd.	Staccato	Play the notes with separation.
		Stagger breathing	Players breathe at different times so the phrase is not broken.
		Style Mark	Indicates the manner or style in which music is to be played.
Flat ♭	Lowers the note and remains in effect the entire measure.		
		Swing	A style of music in which eighth notes are played as if they were written:
forte **f**	Play loudly.		
fortissimo **ff**	Play very loudly.		
Giocosso	Lightly, happily.	Tempo di valse	Waltz tempo.
Grace Note ♪	A small note played on or slightly before the beat.	Tempo	The speed of music.
		Tenuto	Play notes for their full value.
Grazioso	Gracefully.	Time Signature (Meter)	Tells how many beats are in each measure and what kind of note gets one beat.
Half-step	The smallest distance between two notes.		
Harmonic Minor Scale	Like the natural minor scale, except the 7th scale step is raised one half-step.	Treble Clef	"G" clef used by flute, oboe, clarinet, sax, trumpet, and horn.
Interval	The numerical distance between two notes.	Trill	Rapid alternation between two adjacent notes.
Jazz	American form of music combining African and European styles.	Triplet	Group of three notes.
		Unison *unis.*	Tells performers to play the same note.
Key Signature	Flats or sharps next to the clef that apply to the entire piece.		
Legato	Play in a smooth and connected style.	Waltz	Dance in moderate $\frac{3}{4}$ meter.